CLIMBING ONTO THE HORSE'S BACK

CLIMBING ONTO THE HORSE'S BACK

John Zeaman

WITHDRAWN

Before They Were Pets

FRANKLIN WATTS
A Division of Grolier Publishing
New York London Hong Kong Sydney
Danbury, Connecticut

Cover and interior design by Robin Hoffman
Illustrations pp. 12, 21 by Karen Kuchar
Illustrations pp. 17, 24, 27, 47, 52 by Stephen Savage

Photographs ©: Animals Animals: 39, 46, cover insets (Fred Whitehead);
Art Resource: 33 (Werner Forman), 9 (Giraudon), cover, (Mazonowicz),
26 (Nimatallah), 53 (Scala); Musee des Antiquites Nationales: 18; Peter
Arnold Inc.: 40 (Gerard Lacz), 23 (Fretz Prenzel), 41 (Galen Rowell);
Photo Researchers: 12 (Tom McHugh), 42 (Maek Newman), 48 (Gerard
Vandystad), 50 (Roger Wilmshurst); Superstock, Inc.: 43 (The Huntington
library, Art Collections, and Botanical Gardens), 15, 19, 32; The Bridge-
man Art Library International: 10, 25, 30, 34, 35; Tony Stone Images:
55 (Ken Fisher), 2 (Kevin R. Morris), 49 (Gary Mortimore);
Visuals Unlimited: 13.

Visit Franklin Watts on the Internet at:
http://publishing.grolier.com

Library of Congress Cataloging-in-Publication Data

Zeaman, John.
Climbing onto the horse's back / John Zeaman.
p. cm.—(Before they were pets)
Includes bibliographical references (p. 59) and index.
Summary: Surveys the evolution and domestication of horses and
discusses various breeds.
ISBN 0-531-20349-2
1. Horses—Juvenile literature. 2. Equus—Juvenile literature.
3. Horse breeds—Juvenile literature. [1. Horses. 2. Horse breeds.]
I. Title. II. Series: Zeaman, John. Before they were pets.
SF302.Z425 1998
636.1—dc21   97-28659
                                                                        CIP
                                                                         AC

Horses have been one of humanity's greatest friends.

INTRODUCTION

Almost 6,000 years ago, small farming villages covered the vast, grassy plains of eastern Europe. In one of these villages, a 14-year-old boy approaches a fenced corral where several horses are kept. He is about to try something never done before.

These horses don't look like the horses we know today. They are smaller, like large ponies, and they have stiff, upright manes, like zebras. They are kept for their milk, their meat, and their hides—but not for riding. Only gentler animals, such as oxen and asses, are ridden; horses are considered too wild and unpredictable.

But this boy has been raising a mare from birth and has formed a close, affectionate relationship with her. He has spent hours grooming her, pampering her, and feeding her morsels. And, very gradually, the horse has become used to feeling his weight on her back.

Today, as he has done many times before, he slips a small strip of leather over her head and leans across her back. The horse whinnies nervously, but this time the boy goes a step further and slowly slips one leg over the animal. The horse rears back, but the boy holds tight. The frightened horse takes off across the corral, bucking and twisting in an effort to shake the boy off. After a ride of less than a minute, the boy is thrown to the ground. He gets up and wipes the blood from his nose. Several of the village elders have noticed and are pointing at him curiously. He'd done it! Next time, he'd stay on longer.

The Unicorn

The unicorn is an imaginary horselike creature with a horn in the center of its head. It often appears in folktales and legends as a symbol of purity.

No one knows exactly who tamed the first horse for riding, but scientists believe that it happened in a time and place similar to the description above. They also agree that the event was an important event in human history. It was comparable to the invention of the bow and arrow or the sailing ship. Horse and rider became partners, moving and functioning as a unit, with greater abilities than either had alone.

A person on horseback looms 8 feet (2.4 m) tall and can easily outrun any person on foot. On horseback a person can travel quickly from one place to another—bringing news, assistance, or goods. A man and horse are also a formidable fighting machine. Most of the great battles of ancient times were won by the army with the most horses. Genghis Kahn, the mighty Mongol conqueror of the twelfth century, won a great empire with his horseriding

Learning to ride horses was a very important event in human history. This ancient Chinese statue is of a man and his horse.

forces. The tribesmen who fought with him were "born to the saddle," and no army could stop them as they swept across Asia and Central Europe.

In our modern world, horses do not play the central role they once did. They are still used in the American West to herd cattle, and in many cities mounted policemen use horses to keep order. They are also a familiar site in large cities, such as New York, where they pull carriages for tourists. But they are mostly kept for sport and recreation—they have become pets. They are impractical pets for most people, but those who do keep horses know that riding creates an intense bond between horse and human.

In fact, it is said that when the Spanish explorers landed in North America, the American Indians at first thought that horse and man were one, some new godlike being. In Greek mythology there is a creature called the **centaur**—part man, part horse. The fact that people imagined combining themselves with a horse demonstrates the close connection we feel with this animal.

The centaur was a popular figure in Greek mythology.

1

EVOLUTION OF THE MODERN HORSE

Horses belong to a very old family. The earliest known ancestor of the modern horse is called *Hyracotherium*. It roamed the forests of North America and Europe about 60 million years ago. Scientists know what it looked like from petrified remains called **fossils**. It was a small creature, about the size of a fox or a medium-sized dog. It had a much shorter neck than today's horse, and although its slender legs resemble a horse's, *Hyracotherium* had big clumsy feet that looked like paws. There were four toes on each front foot and three on each back foot. These minia-ture, horselike animals eventually evolved into a larger animal with only three toes called the *Mesohippus*.

The Horse Family

All horses belong to the genus Equus. This group also includes asses, zebras, donkeys and mules. All equids have long legs, hoofed feet, flowing tails and a mane on the upper part of the neck.

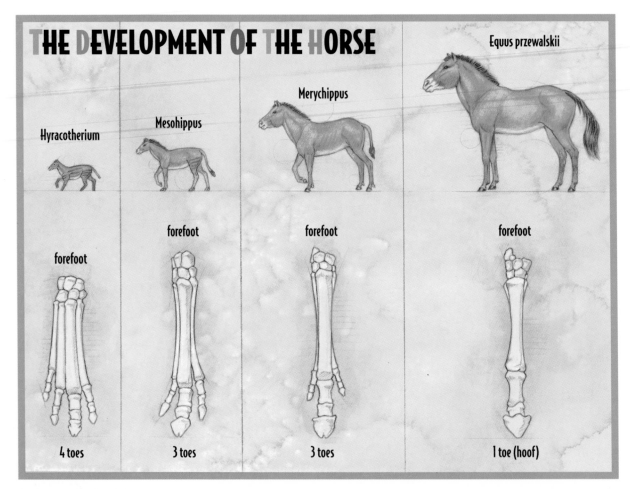

THE DEVELOPMENT OF THE HORSE

Equus przewalskii

Merychippus

Mesohippus

Hyracotherium

forefoot

forefoot

forefoot

forefoot

4 toes

3 toes

3 toes

1 toe (hoof)

As horses evolved into bigger animals, their foot changed from four toes (left) to one toe (right).

During the next 40 million years, horses became larger and larger. They had straighter backs and longer and straighter legs. Their brains grew bigger. Their teeth became longer and harder, allowing horses to chew tough grasses. Their toes changed radically—the middle toe became larger, and the side toes became smaller and smaller until they disappeared. Finally, each foot had only one toe, which ended in an enlarged thick toenail—the only part that touches the ground—called the hoof. This evolutionary change was an incredibly slow process.

This model of a *Mesohippus* is part of a diorama at the Field Museum in Chicago. *Mesohippus*, which lived about 35 million years ago, had three toes.

Horse's feet

Horses hooves are made of bone. The foot also has a pad on the sole of the hoof called the frog. The frog acts like a shock absorber when the horse runs. People put metal horseshoes on a horse's hooves to protect them on hard roads and rough ground.

By about 3 million years ago, horses looked fairly similar to the modern horse. They began to spread across the North American continent. Some went southward to the Isthmus of Panama, where they crossed into South America. Others roamed into Canada and Alaska. At that time,

North America was connected to Asia by a tiny strip of land called the Bering Land Bridge. The horses crossed that about 1 million years ago and spread into Asia. From Asia they went into Africa and Europe. Soon, horses inhabited every continent except Antarctica and Australia.

These animals still did not look like the horses we know today. Some were tall, but others were only 3 feet (0.9 m) high. One group, whose ears grew long, became the animals we now know as asses and donkeys. Others developed stripes and evolved into zebras. Toward the end of the last ice age, huge herds of wild horses roamed the open plains of Europe, Asia, and North America.

EARLY HORSE HUNTERS

During the ice age, humans looked very much like they do today, but they lived very different lives. They lived in caves or rude brush shelters. They hadn't learned how to farm yet. Instead, they gathered nuts and berries. Using stone-tipped spears, they also hunted bison, reindeer, mammoths, and horses.

Archaeologists realized that early humans ate horses after discovering horse bones around the sites of primitive huts. Archaeologists have also found places where ancient hunters stampeded horses off cliffs. In France, near the modern village of Solutre, archaeologists uncovered a 13,000-year-old killing site where prehistoric hunters slaughtered more than 100,000 horses.

These prehistoric people left another record of their relationship with horses: beautiful cave paintings of fat, prancing steeds or small, shaggy ponies with bushy tails. Archaeologists suspect that these pictures were part of a magic ritual to help bring success in hunting. Today, these

14

Early humans painted pictures of horses on the walls of caves.

14,000-year-old paintings at Lascaux, France; Altamira, Spain; and other European sites are admired as great works of art.

END OF THE ICE AGE

About 11,000 years ago, Earth's climate grew warmer, bringing the ice age to an end. Giant ice fields, called **glaciers,** melted, causing the oceans to rise. Formations

15

Horse Names

An adult male horse is called a stallion; an adult female is called a mare. Newborn horses are called foals. Young males are called colts; young females are fillies.

such as the Bering Land Bridge were covered by ocean. The warming also caused forests and prairies to appear in places that had previously been too cold, while grasslands that had flourished in cool temperatures began to dry up and wither away. Animals that had been well adapted to the ice-age climate, such as the woolly mammoth and the saber-toothed tiger, died out.

Horses were also affected by the warming. In North and South America, their numbers began to decrease. No one knows why, but by 9000 B.C. all the horses on these two continents had died out. Perhaps humans hunted them into extinction or the climate change made food scarce.

Meanwhile, on the other side of the Atlantic Ocean, horses in Western Europe were also threatened. Forests spread across what is now Germany and France, and horses had to migrate east in search of new pastures. They eventually made their home on the **steppes,** the grasslands of southern Russia and west-central Asia. By 3000 B.C., these Eurasian prairies had become the horse's principal home.

2

DOMESTICATION OF THE HORSE

No one knows exactly when the horse was first tamed. One curious piece of evidence has puzzled archaeologists for almost 100 years. It is a tiny ivory carving of a horse's head from a cave in the French Pyrenees mountain range. It was made during the **Paleolithic** period, between 10,000 and 14,000 years ago. The dotted markings on this head make it appear that the animal is wearing a rope bridle.

Some scientists have argued that this is proof that the horse was tamed more than 14,000 years ago. But others disagree. They reason that even if early humans tied

A carving much like this one has led many archaeologists to argue that humans tamed horses more than 14,000 years ago.

horses up, it does not prove that they had truly tamed them. Still other scientists say that the lines on the ivory head don't show a bridle at all. The lines were simply the artist's way of showing the white muzzle and other facial markings of early horses.

HORSE VISION

The horse has one of the biggest eyes in the **mammal** kingdom. Because a horse's eye bulges out so far, and because the eyes are located on the sides of the head, the horse has a huge range of vision. It can see almost completely around it, except for two small blind spots immediately in front of and behind its body. That is why a horse can be badly startled if someone approaches it from these angles.

Horses have good night vision and can see much better than their riders at night. A horse is also very good at picking up tiny movements in the distance. In one test, horses were able to recognize their owners in a group of people more than 1,300 feet (396 m) away.

It took humans hundreds of years to learn how to ride horses.

Most scientists agree that the taming of the horse happened by 4000 B.C. By this time, the farmers of the steppes had already tamed wolves, pigs, sheep, goats, and cattle. But horses were more difficult to capture and keep than any of these animals. Horses can be very unpredictable. In the wild, they are hunted by wolves or large cats. They survive by their speed, and by nature they are nervous, skittish, and quick to flight.

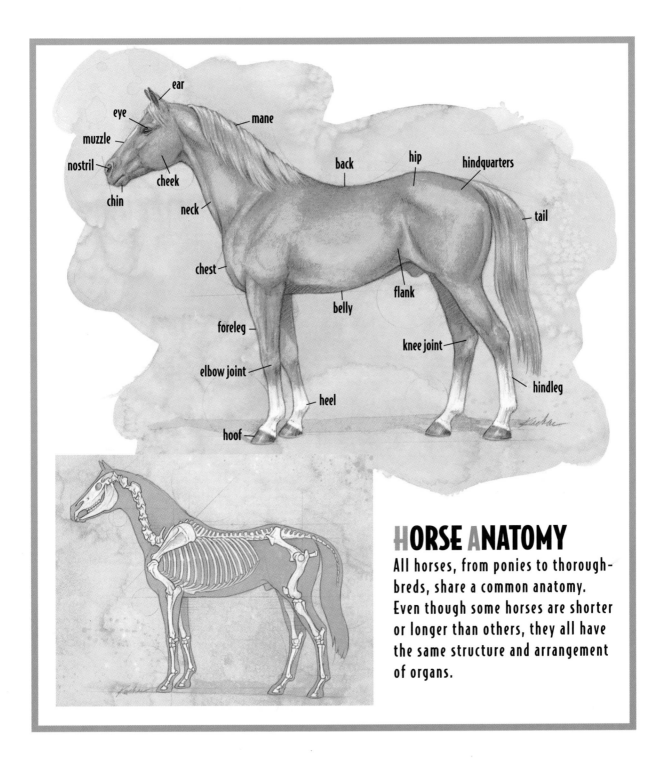

ear

eye

mane

muzzle

nostril

back

hip

hindquarters

cheek

chin

tail

neck

chest

flank

belly

foreleg

knee joint

elbow joint

hindleg

heel

hoof

HORSE ANATOMY

All horses, from ponies to thoroughbreds, share a common anatomy.
Even though some horses are shorter
or longer than others, they all have
the same structure and arrangement
of organs.

How Long is a Horse's Tail?

Shorter than it looks. The hair that grows on the tails of horses is very long. But if you cut away the hair, you would see that the tail itself is short—no more than 15 inches long (38 cm) on the average.

It's no wonder that it took people so long to learn to ride them. An untamed horse panics when anything gets on its back, because that's how it is often attacked in the wild. This wildness remains in the horse's personality to this day. A horse can never be made as tame and as intensely loyal as a dog. Even after thousands of years of **breeding**, every individual horse must be tamed for riding.

How then, with such nervous temperaments, have horses been made to serve people so well? How is it that horses and people can have such close, affectionate relationships?

SOCIABLE ANIMALS

The reason the horse has been able to bond with people lies in the other side of the horse's personality—its sociability. Horses are herd animals. They live in small groups where cooperation is instinctive and necessary for survival. They are extremely friendly with one another. Horses form close friendships with other horses, especially their siblings, and demonstrate affection by grooming each other's manes or swishing flies off each other with their tails.

Grooming, or brushing and cleaning a horse, is a very important part of the taming process. When people groom horses, they do much more than simply make the horse look neat and tidy. In the horse's mind, being groomed by a person is a sign that the human companion is its close friend. Grooming makes the horse eager to please the person and much more cooperative when it is being ridden.

Once horses began to be born and raised in captivity, they started to bond with people. They felt the same feel-

ings toward people that they felt toward other horses. The taming process had begun.

PHYSICAL CHANGES

How did horses evolve into different shapes and sizes? The horses that came from the Eurasian steppes looked like stocky ponies. Those from Egypt and Arabia were more slender, with longer legs. Scientists believe that this difference reflects the way horses evolved in different climates. Over thousands of years, animals that live in colder climates tend to become smaller and more compact, because that body resists the cold better. The animals that live in hot climates, such as Egypt, became thinner, a body type that allows them to cool off quickly. Today, scientists refer to these different horses by their places of origin, such as the Arabian horse, the Steppe horse, the Forest horse, and the Plateau horse.

PUTTING THE HORSE TO WORK

As people succeeded in taming horses, they began to wonder if this animal would carry things or pull a cart. Oxen and asses were already used in this way, but these animals were slow and sometimes uncooperative. Horses were a bit unpredictable, perhaps, but they were smart and fast. Archaeologists believe that horses were hitched up to carts by 3500 B.C. because they have found horse bones and bits of harness dating to this time at several sites on the steppes.

For a long time, only Eurasian people knew about tamed horses. The vast grasslands they inhabited were thousands of miles from other centers of civilization. There was little or no contact with people of other lands, many of whom had never seen a horse.

When horses were first brought to Mesopotamia around 2000 B.C., the people there saw them as new and strange animals,

24

An Egyptian king charges into battle in a horse-drawn chariot.

which they called *ansekurra*, or the "the ass from foreign lands." Within a short time, they, too, had begun to use horses in place of oxen and asses.

All over the civilized world, people began taming and using horses. By 1500 B.C., warriors in Egypt, Greece, and India were riding off to battle in horse-drawn chariots. In 1300 B.C., a Chinese king was buried alongside his favorite steeds. By 950 B.C., King Solomon of Israel had a stable of 12,000 horses.

25

STARTING TO RIDE

But when exactly did people climb up onto the horse's back? When did they become true riders? This is a difficult puzzle for archaeologists to solve, because the first riders probably used nothing more than a simple harness. Equipment like saddles and stirrups took a long time to develop, and the first riders would not have left much evidence for archaeologists to dig up. However, most scientists believe that it probably happened between 3000 B.C. and 2000 B.C.

This Egyptian rider sits uncomfortably on the rear of the horse.

The earliest proof of riding is a wooden figure of a man on a horse that was discovered in an Egyptian tomb from 1350 B.C. Also, Egyptian battle scenes from 1300 B.C. show a few men on horseback. In both cases, the riders are shown perched awkwardly far back on the rump of the horse. They had not yet become skillful riders.

3

BREEDING A LARGER HORSE

Once people began to ride horses, they began to consider how to make them bigger and faster. All the horses of the ancient world were fairly small. Most were less than 14 hands (4.7 feet or 1.4 m) at the shoulder, and many were only 12 hands (4 feet or 1.2 m)—about the size of a Shetland pony. The breeding of larger horses is believed to have begun on the Eurasian steppes, among a group of people called the Scythians.

THE SCYTHIANS

Elsewhere in the world the changes caused by tamed horses were slow, but not in Scythia. These Eurasian tribal people rode off on their horses and never looked back. In about 900 B.C., with a suddenness that still surprises archaeologists, they began to abandon their villages and farms. Instead of growing food, they used horses to track big, swift animals such as elk and bison. They drove huge herds of cattle across the vast prairies. Their homes became tents; their hearth was a campfire under the sky.

They used horses in every imaginable way. They ate horsemeat and drank mare's milk. Their favorite drink was a liquor called *koumiss*, which was made out of fermented mare's milk. Their leather goods were made of horsehide, and their ropes were twisted horsehair. Even their clothing was designed for horseback riding. Instead of sandals and robes, these mounted **nomads** put on trousers and boots.

The Scythians learned to increase the size of their horses by taking better care of them. Instead of letting them eat on their own during the winter, when food was scarce, they fed their horses grains and gave them shelter. The horses grew healthier and bigger. After several generations, these well-cared-for mounts stood inches taller than wild horses.

With their skill in riding, the Scythians could also capture the biggest and strongest wild horses from among the vast herds that roamed the steppes. They took these superior horses and bred them together, repeating the process over hundreds of generations until they had created the kind of horse that suited them.

How Horses are Measured

Horses are measured in "hands" from the ground to the withers (the highest point of the shoulder). One hand equals 4 inches (10 cm). Shire horses are the largest (up to 18 hands) and Shetland ponies are the smallest (12 hands).

This ancient Greek bracelet shows two Scythian horsemen.

Even after breeding, the Scythian horses were not large—nothing like the hefty Clydesdales or long-legged thoroughbreds we are familiar with today. From ancient Scythian pictures, we know that Scythian horses were compact and well-muscled, like very strong-looking ponies. They were the best horses of that time. Over the centuries, great numbers of Scythian horses were imported into Greece. It is also likely that the large Roman military horses were bred from stock that came originally from Scythia.

CONQUERING HORDES

All across the vast steppes other peoples—the Sarmatians, the Huns, and the Mongols—were creating a life similar to that of the Scythians. Soon these people would change history.

Tribes began to compete with each other and to form alliances. Gradually their numbers swelled until they were no longer tribes, but huge groups. As they advanced to the edges of the steppes, they overran the settled peoples living on villages and farms. They stole cattle and demanded payments of grain or other food. The farmers had no choice but to obey. The horses must have seemed extremely frightening to an ordinary farmer at that time.

Eventually, the people of the settled cities took measures to protect themselves from these fierce horsemen. The most famous example is the Great Wall of China, which was completed in 214 B.C. to keep out the Huns. The wall kept the Huns out of China, but they continued to grow in power, and other peoples were not so successful in stopping them. In A.D. 452, under the leadership of their great general Attila, the Huns invaded Italy and helped destroy the Roman Empire.

About 700 years later, another tribe of wandering horsemen, the Mongols, rose to power. In 1206, their chieftain, Genghis Khan, led his cavalry down from the steppes, sweeping across Asia and building the greatest land empire ever known. By 1279, Khan's empire stretched from the Pacific coast of Asia to the Black Sea. The reason for the Mongols' success was simple. They had good strong horses and rode them skillfully. They attacked quickly and fled. No one could catch them. Mongol cavalrymen sprinted across country at an extraordinary rate, covering as many as 90 miles (145 km) in a single day.

The Great Wall of China was built to keep out the horsemen of eastern Asia.

Living off their Horses

Mongol warriors often used their horses as a source of emergency nourishment. On a long journey, a soldier mixed dried mare's milk with water and gulped it down for breakfast. Sometimes they would drain a cupful of blood from their horse's veins and drink that. They could do this once every 10 days without harming the horse.

In this painting, Genghis Khan's horsemen ride into battle.

GREAT HORSES

For at least 1,000 years, horseback riders clung to their horses with their legs. This required great skill and balance and made it difficult for warriors to throw spears or shoot arrows accurately. Once again, this problem was solved by the Scythians. A gold collar from the fourth cen-

How Horses Run

Horses move at four different speeds. They can walk, trot, canter, or gallop. When a horse gallops, all four of its hooves are off the ground for a split second during each stride.

tury B.C. shows men riding with loops around their feet. This is the first evidence that people had begun to use stirrups. Their use gradually spread through the Roman Empire, but stirrups did not reach western Europe until the eighth century A.D.

By that time, a new kind of horseman existed in Europe—the armored knight. At first, these knights wore fairly lightweight suits of flexible armor and their horses did not need to be especially large. By 1300, however,

While a king and queen watch, two knights joust each other at a tournament.

HORSE MESSENGERS

Cyrus the Great, a Persian king, established the horse messenger service 2,400 years ago. He created a system of relay stations to carry letters across his vast empire. Each relay station was 15 miles (24 km) apart. There, the horseman exchanged his tired horse for a fresh one. The Persian couriers could travel 180 miles (290 km) in a single day. Later, this same system was used by the Romans and by Arab sultans. The most famous horse-powered postal system was the Pony Express, started in 1860 to transport mail across the American west. It took 11 days for a series of riders to travel 2,000 miles (3,218 km), from St. Joseph, Missouri, to Sacramento, California. The Pony Express lasted only 1 year. In 1861, the first transcontinental telegraph line was completed, making it possible to send messages from coast to coast in just a few seconds.

metalsmiths were fashioning heavy, arrow-proof armor out of metal plates. The total weight the horse had to carry—including man, armor, and weapons—often came to 400 pounds (181 kg).

Huge horses were needed to carry such a load. And so breeders created the "Great Horses," or chargers, which became the ancestors of many large modern workhorses such as the Shire and the Percheron. With so much weight on their backs, these horses did not gallop with the speed of the lightly burdened Scythian or Mongol horses. Race horses can go as fast as 40 miles (64 km) an hour, but a

A huge horse was needed to carry an armored knight into battle.

horse with an armored knight probably charged at the ponderous rate of 10 or 12 miles (16 or 19 km) an hour.

In medieval battles and tournaments, strength, not speed, was the important factor. Knights on horseback charged each other with long lances, trying to knock an opponent off his horse. In battle, a knight without a horse was usually doomed.

Eventually, however, armor became obsolete. Knights on horseback were simply too slow and unable to maneuver as well as lighter cavalry. Beginning in the 1300s, cannon and other firearms were invented. Steel suits couldn't stop bullets. Generals also began to realize that soldiers on foot could aim guns better than men on horseback. New tactics grouped foot soldiers into squares. The foot soldiers were protected on all sides because horses won't run into a line of men that doesn't scatter.

Horses continued to be used in warfare right up into the twentieth century, when they were replaced by tanks, trucks, and helicopters. The days when battles are decided by the cavalry are over.

Horses through the Ages

More than 250 different types of horses have lived on Earth since Hyracotherium appeared about 60 million years ago. Most of the horse's ancestors were striped or spotted.

CHAPTER 4

THE WILD HORSE TODAY

Some scientists believe that horses might have become extinct if people hadn't **domesticated** them. Wild horses had already died out in the Americas and were dwindling in Europe. By taming them and bringing them all over the world, people may have saved the **species.**

But what happened to the original wild horses? Did any of them survive?

One species of wild horse was the *tarpan*, which lived on the steppes of the Ukraine. Sadly, the last one died in a Polish zoo in 1851. Tarpans were smaller and stockier than today's horses, and, like the zebra, had a stiff, erect mane rather than the flowing mane of today's horse.

Modern scientists, however, have not been content to let the tarpan go extinct. They have reasoned that the tarpan's **genes** still exist in the modern horse today. They studied the bones of the tarpan and learned everything they could about its appearance. Then they set out, by **selective breeding,** to recreate the wild horse. Gradually, over many generations, a horse emerged that scientists call a **reconstituted** tarpan. It has all the features of a tarpan—the size, bone structure, and stiff mane. But since it was artificially bred, it cannot be called a true tarpan.

Two tarpan mares groom each other.

PRZEWALSKI'S HORSE

After the death of the last tarpan, it was believed that the wild horse had become truly extinct. Then, in 1870, a Russian explorer named Nikolai Przewalski spotted a herd of yellow horses along the border of China and Mongolia. After

Przewalski discovered this species of horses roaming through Mongolia.

zoological expeditions captured them, it was determined that these animals could not have escaped from local tribesmen. Like tarpans, they had primitive, erect manes.

They were the last survivors of the huge herds that had once roamed the vast steppes. For many years, these animals regularly grazed near Takhin Shar-nuru, the Mountain of Yellow Horses, in Mongolia. But in 1977, the herd was not seen in its usual pasture, and it has not been seen since.

Fortunately, these Przewalski's horses (as they are now called) are bred in zoos all over the world for future release into the wild. In 1994, twenty were sent to Mongolia, where they once again run free.

What of the wild horses that live in the American West? How did they come to be here?

These are not true wild horses. They are the descendants of domesticated horses brought here by European explorers and settlers. Christopher Columbus brought twenty horses with him when he landed in the New World in 1492. These were the first horses to set foot in the Americas since 9000 B.C. Later, Spanish explorers brought with them a horse called the jennet, a **breed** created from Arabian and European horses. Eventually, many of these horses escaped into the wild and multiplied on the western plains of North America and on the pampas, or prairies, of South America.

These **feral** horses came to be called mustangs, from the Spanish word *mestenos*, or "strayed ones." These mustangs are actually somewhat smaller than the domestic horses they are descended from. Horses that are well fed and cared for by people generally increase in size over several generations. Horses returned to the wild become smaller.

Wild horses were brought to North and South America by Spanish explorers in the 1500s.

Centuries ago, some 2 million of these wild horses roamed the western plains. American Indians tamed thousands of them, changing the Indians' lives completely. Within a short span of only 40 years, tribes that had scratched out a living as primitive farmers and as hunters and fishers on foot were suddenly transformed. They rode

HORSE SOCIETY IN THE WILD

In the wild, horses live in herds that range in size from two to thirty individuals, but most groups have between three and seven animals. A typical group consists of a mature stallion, his mares, and their foals. The stallion will not let any other male horses join his group. When the young males, the colts, are about 18 months old, the stallion will usually drive them away. These colts go off and join a group of other young males until they can start their own herd. The stallion is not the leader of the herd in every situation. Often it is the mares who decide which way the herd will go, and the stallion trails along behind, keeping the herd together.

The horse allowed American Indians to chase and hunt buffalo.

deep into the American prairies pursuing the buffalo. They too became nomads and proud warriors. The horse had carried them into a new life.

44

CHAPTER 5 HORSE BREEDS

Today, there are three main groups of horses: ponies, light horses, and draft horses.

PONIES

A pony is any horse that is less than 58 inches (147 cm) tall, although height is not the only thing that makes ponies different from horses. Ponies are similar to the early ancestors of horses and to those ridden by the people of the steppes. They have short legs and a sturdy body. Pound for pound, they are stronger than horses.

Oldest Breed

The oldest breed of horse in the world is the spotted Appaloosa, which has six basic patterns. It originated in China and is believed to be at least 3,000 years old.

Three Shetland ponies

Today there are sixty-seven types of ponies. The Shetland pony has lived on the islands north of Scotland since ancient times. Shetlands range from 38 to 48 inches (97 to 122 cm) tall. Shetland ponies are stocky animals. They look like tiny draft horses with thick bodies, sturdy legs, and strong muscles. In Scotland, these ponies pull small carts or carry heavy loads on their backs. In North America, they are ridden or driven by children, and they perform in circuses.

The Falabella is a different kind of pony. It is smaller than the Shetland, but it has the proportions of a horse. Some people refer to it as a miniature horse. These horses are too small to ride and are kept purely as exotic pets. Their average height is only 34 inches (86 cm), which makes them smaller than many breeds of dog. The tiniest adult Falabella is only 15 inches (38 cm) at the shoulder.

Perhaps you're wondering how such a large animal as the horse can be bred so small. The tiny *Hyracotherium* was only 10 inches (25 cm) high. We can see the Falabella as a specimen that recalls the horse's origins some 60 million years ago.

LIGHT HORSES

Light breeds are the largest and most varied group of horses. Almost all of the 104 types of light horses are partly descended from the Arabian, a horse that was bred in central Arabia in ancient times. This type of horse is often black, although it can be any color. It is small, standing about 58 inches (147 cm) and weighing 800 to 900 pounds (363 to 408 kg). Arabians are not particularly fast, but they have great endurance.

Light horses are used for sports and recreation, such as polo.

Light horses are also called sporting horses because they are used for many recreational purposes, such as riding, hunting, racing, show-jumping, and polo.

Horse racing probably dates back to the beginning of riding. The earliest recorded reference to it comes from 1730 B.C., when the Mesopotamian king Samsi-adad ordered his son to send racing chariots to the city of Assur for the New Year's festival. Chariot racing flourished in Greece and ancient Rome. Today, the equivalent of chariot racing is harness racing, for which the harness horse has been bred.

The other kind of horse racing, in which horses run with jockeys on their backs, became popular in seventeenth-century England. The thoroughbred was bred for this. It stands about 60 to 65 inches (152 to 165 cm) and weighs from 1,000 to 1,250 pounds (454 to 567 kg). A thoroughbred can gallop about 30 miles an hour (48 km/hr)

Due to their speed, thoroughbreds are used in races.

over vast distances. A horse similar to the thoroughbred, called the quarterhorse, sprints in short races and reaches speeds of 40 miles an hour (64 km/hr). Today, this breed is popular on cattle ranches, where it makes a fine "cow pony."

DRAFT HORSES

The draft horses are the giants of the horse world. Among the thirty-six types are the Shire, the Percheron, and the

Huge horses, such as these Shires, were traditionally used to perform heavy labor.

Clydesdale. They are the descendants of the horses ridden by the knights of northern and western Europe. Some have stood more than 7 feet (2.1 m) at the shoulder and have weighed more than a ton. These were the horses that pulled plows and wagons in the days before trucks, cars, and tractors. Today, these horses have become show animals at county fairs, parades, or horse shows.

CHAPTER 6

HORSES AS PETS

Horses aren't the important animals they once were. Machines have replaced them as work animals. They no longer gallop off to war. Children who grow up in cities may never see a horse.

Although the horse has lost its central role in human society and it no longer makes history, it probably enjoys a better life today than it did in the past.

People have not always been kind to horses. The zoologist and writer Desmond Morris once described the horse as "man's

This ancient statue shows the majesty and power of the horse in the human imagination.

How Long Do Horses Live?

Most horses live about 20 to 25 years. A working horse is considered old at 17 years. The record lifespan for a horse is 62 years. (This horse, named Old Billy, lived in England in the 1700s.)

best slave." Throughout history, horses have been harnessed, ridden, spurred, and whipped. They have been forced to pull heavy loads all day with no reward other than a bag of feed. Millions of horses have been ridden into bloody battlefields where they were hacked to pieces or blown apart by cannon fire.

Only the dog and the horse show such blind devotion to people. Imagine how a cat would react if you put a load on its back or tried to hook it up to a harness. No amount of training would convince a cat to do that.

The horse feels a special bond with people, which comes from its naturally sociable lifestyle in the wild. People, in turn, feel intense affection and admiration for horses. No other animal has inspired so much art or poetry. People love to describe the horse's spirit, grace, strength, and nobility. Those admirable qualities, including its willingness to serve people, make the horse a very special animal indeed.

Now that they are no longer seen as work animals or as creatures to be exploited, people lavish more care and devotion on horses than ever before.

Few people can keep horses purely as pets. They are expensive to buy and to keep. They require their own living quarters and a corral or pasture in which to exercise. They cannot be allowed to roam on their own like a cat or be walked down a city sidewalk like a dog.

Perhaps the breeding of smaller horses, like the tiny Falabella, will make it possible for more people to keep horses. But even this horse cannot be housebroken like a dog or a cat and hence cannot share our homes with us.

But people who are lucky enough to be able to keep horses feel a bond and connection to them that is unsurpassed by any other companion animal.

For both people and horses, their exists a special bond of friendship that is thousands of years old.

GLOSSARY

archaeology   The study of the way humans or animals lived a very long time ago. Archaeologists dig up the remains of ancient cities or settlements and study the bones, weapons, pottery, and other things they find. They also dig up the remains of animals and study their bones to understand how they lived and changed over time.

breed   A group of animals that have been changed by people. A breed is created by picking specific animals to mate and have offspring. As a result these animals have a particular uniform appearance, as in the case of such horses as thoroughbreds, Shetland ponies, or Clydesdales.

centaur   A creature in Greek legend that was part man and part horse.

conquistadors   The Spanish conquerors of Mexico, Peru, or other parts of the Americas in the 1500s.

domestication   The act of training or changing a wild animal so that it can be used by people.

equus   The genus that horses, zebras, donkeys, mules, and asses belong to.

feral   A wild animal, particularly one that was formerly tame or domesticated.

fossil   The remains of a plant or animal from millions of years ago preserved in rock.

genes   The tiny units of a cell of an animal or plant that determine the characteristics that an offspring inherits from its parent or parents.

genus   Classification of plants or animals with common characteristics. Horses, asses, donkeys, mules, and zebras belong to the genus *Equus.*

glacier   A huge sheet of ice found in mountain valleys or polar regions.

nomad   A member of a group or tribe that does not have a permanent home. Nomads wander from place to place looking for food or for land where they can find food for their animals.

nomadic   Wandering from place to place.

paleolithic   A period in the early stone age, about 10,000 to 14,000 years ago, when people lived by hunting, fishing, and gathering plants.

reconstitute   To make over again, or to reconstruct something from parts that have been separated.

selective breeding   To pick specific animals to mate and have offspring in order to create an animal with a particular uniform appearance or behavior.

species   A group of animals or plants, smaller than a genus, that have certain characteristics in common. For example, wild horses belong to the genus *Equus* and the species *ferus*, and scientists refer to them as *Equus ferus*. The mountain zebra is called *Equus zebra*.

steppe   A large grassy plain. Steppes are found in southeastern Europe and parts of Asia.

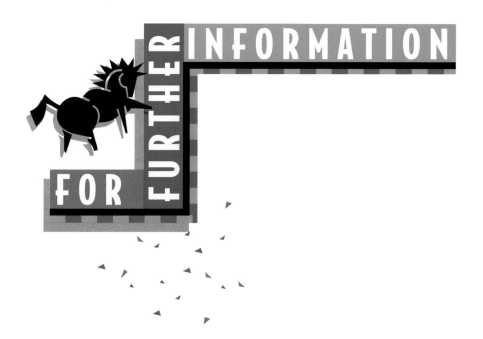

BOOKS

Burns, William A. *Horses and Their Ancestors*. New York: McGraw-Hill, 1954.

Darling, Lois, and Louis Darling. *Sixty Million Years of Horses.* Morrow Junior Books, 1960

Ipcar, Dahlov. *Horses of Long Ago*. Garden City, New York: Doubleday and Co., 1965.

Jurmain, Suzanne. *Once Upon A Horse: A History of Horses and How They Shaped Our Culture*. New York: Lothrop, Lee and Shepard, 1989.

Sander, Lenore. *Animals that Work for Man*. Englewood Cliffs, N.J.: Prentice Hall, 1966.

59

Wexo, John Bonnet. *Wild Horses Zoobooks*. November 1991 issue, Volume Nine, Number Two, Wildlife Education Ltd., San Diego, Ca.

Wood, Gerald L. *Guinness Book of Pet Records*. Enfield, Middlesex, Great Britain: Guinness Superlatives Ltd. 1984.

INTERNET SITES

Breed of Livestock–Horses

http://www.ansi.okstate.edu/breeds/horses/

This site provides an in-depth look at the characteristics and history of each horse breed.

Horsefun

http://horsefun.com/

For young horselovers, a wonderful site filled with games, articles, and interesting information about horses.

The Horse Interactive

http://www.thehorse.com/

This is an advanced site devoted to horse health.

Horseland

http://www.horseland.com/

A fun site that features chat rooms and links to other horse pages.

Horses, Horses, & More Horses

http://www.horses.co.uk/

This site features hundreds of photographs of horses jumping, prancing, trotting, etc.

Horse Worldwide

http://www.horseworldwide.com/

A site for horse enthusiasts that includes a chat room and many fine photographs.

INDEX

Page numbers in *italics* indicate illustrations.

ABOUT THE AUTHOR

JOHN ZEAMAN is a journalist. For the past thirteen years, he has been a critic, feature writer, and editor with the *Bergen Record* of New Jersey. His interest in pets and animal domestication stems from the numerous pets that have lived in his household, including a standard poodle, two cats, gerbils, a parakeet, finches, lizards, turtles, a garter snake, and, briefly, a wild squirrel. The idea for this series grew out of a project that his daughter did in the fifth grade on the origins of pets. He lives in Leonia, New Jersey, with his wife, Janet, and their children, Claire and Alex.